Dedicated To
The One I Love

THE SHIRELLES

© Copyright 2019 • Josh Tuininga

All rights reserved. No part of this book may be reproduced or transmitted in any form or by any means, electronic or mechanical, including photocopying, recording, or by any information storage and retrieval system, without written permission from the author.

A NOTE ABOUT FAIR USE

All artist names and song titles are printed in accordance with fair use. Song titles and artist names are not protected under copyright law. The U.S. Copyright Office has never found that a title of any length could be successfully registered for copyright protection.

BLUE BUS PUBLISHING

FOR MORE BOOKS & ART VISIT:
BlueBusArt.com

First Edition
ISBN# 978-0-578-40574-2
Printed in PRC

You're listening to Classic Rock and R&B hits ALL NIGHT LONG!

Our first song tonight is...

CLICK

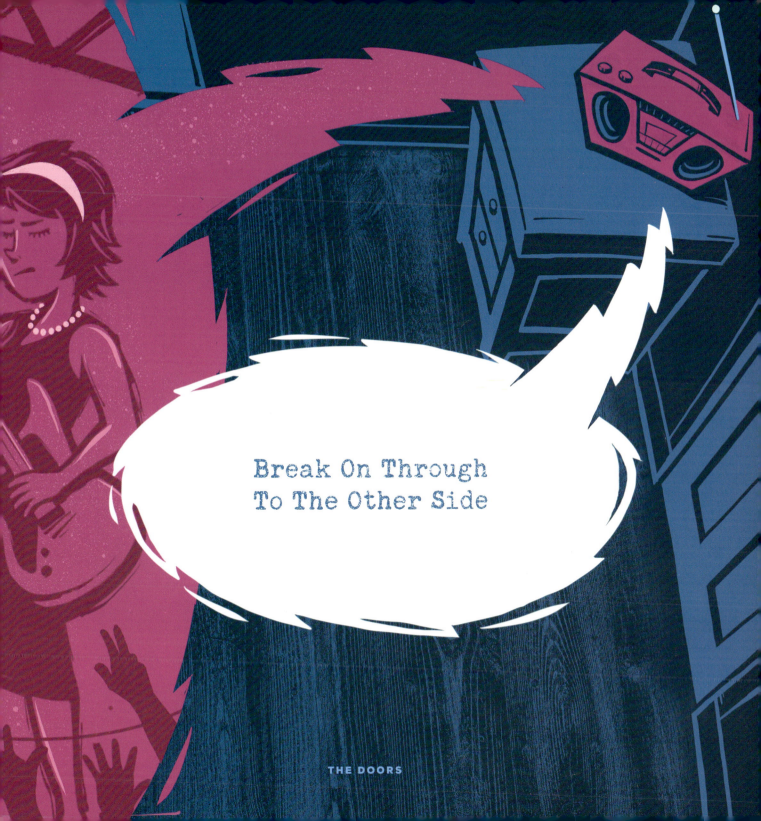

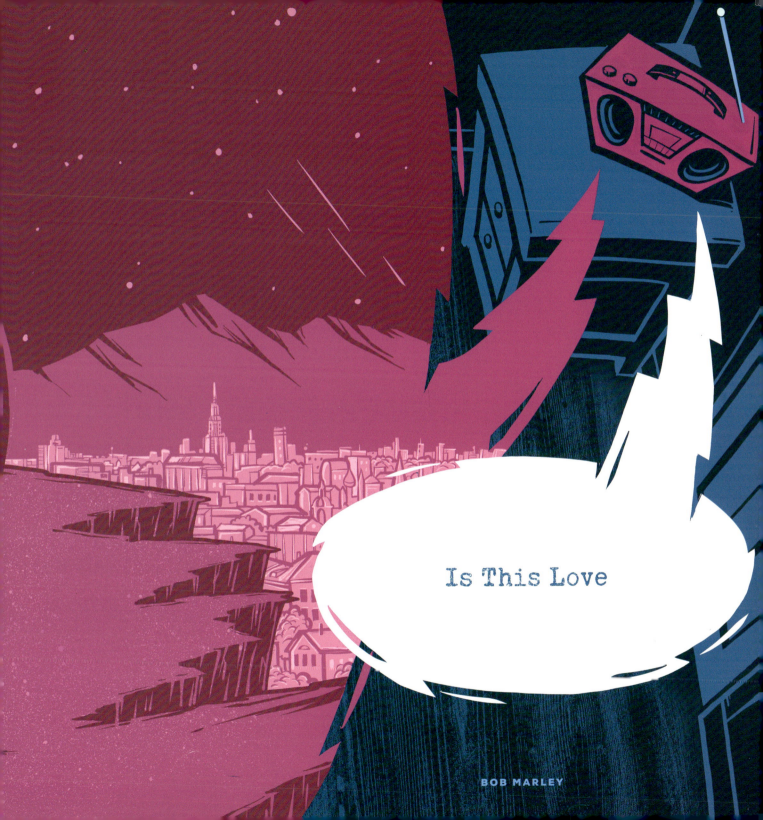

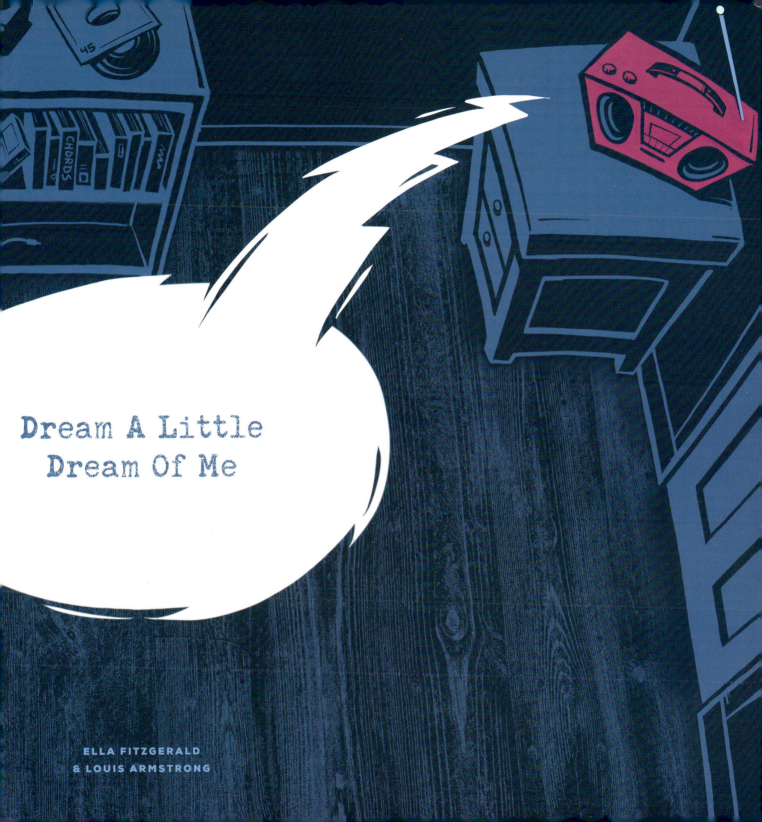

DREAM ON
PLAYLIST

01 Dedicated To The One I Love
THE "5" ROYALES • 1957 | THE SHIRELLES • 1961
THE MAMAS & THE PAPAS • 1967

02 Dream On
AEROSMITH • 1973

03 Under Pressure
QUEEN & DAVID BOWIE • 1981

04 I Won't Back Down
TOM PETTY • 1989

05 With A Little Help From My Friends
THE BEATLES • 1967 | JOE COCKER • 1968

06 All I Have To Do Is Dream
EVERLY BROTHERS • 1958

07 Break On Through To The Other Side
THE DOORS • 1967

08 Dont You Worry 'Bout A Thing
STEVIE WONDER • 1973

09 Set Me Free
THE KINKS • 1965

10 That's All Right, Mama
ARTHUR CRUDUP • 1946 | ELVIS PRESLEY • 1954

11 We Gotta Get Out Of This Place
THE ANIMALS • 1965

12 Wouldn't It Be Nice
THE BEACH BOYS • 1966

13 No Particular Place To Go
CHUCK BERRY • 1964

14 In The Still Of The Night
THE FIVE SATINS • 1956

15 Is This Love
BOB MARLEY & THE WAILERS • 1978

16 Dream A Little Dream Of Me
ELLA FITZGERALD & LOUIS ARMSTRONG • 1950
THE MAMAS & THE PAPAS • 1963
Recorded by over 60 artists including Ozzie Nelson, Nat King Cole,
Doris Day, Dean Martin, Bing Crosby, and Henry Mancini

17 Blowin' In The Wind
BOB DYLAN • 1963 | PETER, PAUL & MARY • 1963

18 Here Comes The Sun
THE BEATLES • 1969 | BOOKER T. & THE M.G.'S • 1970
NINA SIMONE • 1971

19 A Change Is Gonna Come
SAM COOKE • 1964 | OTIS REDDING • 1965 | THE BAND • 1973
THE SUPREMES • 1965 | ARETHA FRANKLIN • 1967

20 I Want You Back
THE JACKSON 5 • 1969

21 Bye, Bye Baby
JANIS JOPLIN • 1967

LISTEN ON SPOTIFY:
spoti.fi/2FZ1jgS

THIS BOOK WAS PUBLISHED THANKS TO SUPPORT FROM:

Drew & Cedar Skillman
& Lydia Choy

Marco Calvo & Nicole Caden

Aaron, Sarika, Anika
& Isaac Singh-Bell

Ryan & Milo Bierman
& Melanie Majerech

Jeff Caden & Debby Halperin

Leon Policar-Comeau

Vinny & Chelsea McKee

Rich & Nancy Bell

Gina & Steve Dichter

Sarah Skinner

Lloy & Steven Schaaf

Tom & Judy Skillman

Kristin Cruse

Darcy Carlson

Ian & Victor Whiteford
& Adrienne Wang

Jocelyn, J.J. &
Hattie Mae Engler

Bernice Kaster

The Russak's

Bill Wagner

Jeff Altaras

Mike, Megan, Amelie
& Isobel Saffitz

Marie Connelly

Winnie Hackett

Beth Burrows

Ricca I. Martin

Cheryl McQuiston

Peter Meyers

Howie & Karli Barokas

Rain City Rock Camp

Mt. Si Montessori

Lisa, Klara, Hazel,
Ron, Barb, Joe, Thea,
Oliver & Ivie Tuininga